                    KIKO
          (voice rising) This can't be
          happening? It's a Monday morning.
          I have a Math test. Will it
          affect my grade point average? My
          parents are going to be so pissed.

                    SUSIE
          It would be helpful to know what
          was happening. Then perhaps we
          could make some kind of plan? Get
          organised. (pause) OMG!. I sound
          just like my Mum.

                    JEM
          The ever practical, Susan Dillon.
          A plan a day keeps the boys away.
          (sniggers) And yes, Thorne or
          Emma or whatever the hell your
          name is this week. I've sent an
          e-mail to the local police and
          Tweeted our predicament. Hey, We
          might start trending soon.

                    BEN
          How can you tweet what's
          happening? We don't even know
          what's going on. It could be
          terrorists or war or anything.

                    THORNE
          Or a zombie apocalypse. It's only
          a matter of time before the undead
          rise to claim bone and blood and
          ash and hair.

Everybody turns to stare at THORNE in amazement. She
hardly ever speaks.

                    THORNE (CONT'D)
          (Looks embarrassed and mutters)
          Well. It is.

                    SUSIE
          I'm going to look through the
          window. We need to know what's
          going on.

SUSIE walks to the class room door and steps onto a desk.
She is still too short so she begins to go on tip toe. All
the other children watch her - alert like meercats.

SUSIE (CONT'D)
(Whispers) It's pretty dark I can't see much. Hold on. There's something... OMG! Oh! Jesus. It's Mrs. Williamson. She's crawling along the floor. Oh! Jesus. Shit. There's blood and ... She's stopped. Just lying still now. I think she's resting.

JEM
Resting? Really. She's covered in blood and she's *resting*. I think we can safely conclude that she is clearly dead. Never did like that bitch anyway. Really patronising.

BEN reaches across and shoves JEM roughly. JEM howls and falls to the floor.

JEM (CONT'D)
Jesus, Ben. You dick head.

BEN
You don't get to talk about people like that. Not in here. Not now. You shut your retarded mouth.

JEM
You got a crush on her, Ben? Mrs. Williams? She's got nice tits.

BEN
SHUT UP!

SUSIE AND THORNE try to pull BEN off JEM but he is so enraged he just throws them off. SUSIE fall against a desk and groans. BEN is distracted and stops his assault on JEM.

BEN (CONT'D)
Susie? I'm really sorry. Are you okay? I didn't mean to hurt you. I just got mad. (pause) I feel frustrated.

THORNE
Dick.

SUSIE
It was an accident. (To JEM) Are you okay?

JEM
Nothing I'm not used to. (Shrugs)

SUSIE
But you completely overreacted, Ben. That's called assault.

JEM
Yeah. I should sue but I can't be arsed.

BEN
I'm sorry. I don't normally do stuff like that. Like violent stuff. This situation is just so weird. And for the record, yes, I do like Mrs. Williamson. She's really cool. Helped me with lots of stuff.

THORNE
What sort of stuff?

BEN
(Pauses) Um, history and... (pause)... decisions. I don't know.

THORNE
But she's an Art Teacher.

JEM
Was an Art Teacher.

Everybody glares at JEM.

BEN
Look, I just like her okay. She was supportive and funny. And shit, is she really dead?

BEN creeps over to the desk and slowly raises himself up.

BEN (CONT'D)
She's not there anymore.

THORNE
She's probably reanimated by now.

(Makes zombie noises and gestures)

> **BEN**
> Jesus. There is a huge blood trail leading up the corridor ...
> (Pause) ... I can see someone coming out of the drama department. I can't see who it is.

A shot rings out and BEN falls off the desk near the body of Mr B. The kids scatter and crouch around the stage except for FANBOY. He remains silent, invisible.

MOTHER enters stage right and stands up-stage right facing the audience.

> **MOTHER**
> I have to go to the school. To pick up my daughter. Sasha, that's my daughter, just called me to tell me that there are kids shooting in the school. Kids are killing other kids. With guns. I could hear this terrible screaming in the background and my head filled with smoke. I feel weightless but trapped and my head, my head doesn't seem to be working properly. I think she said she had been shot. Yes, yes, she said she had been hurt. Oh! God! My child. My beautiful girl. Hurt and I don't know how badly.

Mother exits stage right.

> **SUSIE**
> (Whispers) Ben? Ben? Are you okay?.

> **BEN**
> (Whispers) I'm okay but Mr B isn't looking too good.

> **SUSIE**
> Has he got a pulse?

> **BEN**
> I can't feel one. But I don't really know how to do it. He's very cold. I don't think he's breathing.

INT. Early morning. Classroom

It is 8.40 am and JEM, KIKO, THORNE, BEN, SUSIE, FANBOY are standing/sitting tensely around the classroom. MR B lies prone on the floor. Blood covers his face and shirt. There are 4 desks/tables in the centre of the room. A fire alarm rings and stops abruptly. BEN is crouched by MR B's body.

                    BEN
Mr. B is still bleeding. He looks
really bad.

                    SUSIE
Keep the pressure on the wound.
Why have you taken your hand off?

                    BEN
It makes me feel sick. The blood.
I didn't know it would be so
sticky.

                    SUSIE
You have to apply pressure to the
wound. It will help stop the
bleeding. I can't do anything
about his head. Besides he
screamed really loud when we tried
to turn him ... (Pause) ... I
don't want to try that again.

                    BEN
Where did you learn all this. Are
your parents doctors or something?

                    SUSIE
Grays Anatomy.

                    JEM
Yeah, the lame ass show
responsible for thousands of
amateur medics nationwide.

                    BEN
What the fuck have you done?
Except video Mr. C and post it to
You Tube. Sick bastard.

                    JEM
I'm just recording this event for
history. People will want to know
about it.

                    KIKO
If we survive it.

                    JEM
Well, yeah. (Adopts Dracula
accent) If we live through this
night.

                    KIKO
How can you make jokes? We might
die here. All of us. I wish we
knew what was happening.

                    JEM
I guarantee you its not something
good.

                    THORNE
Can you just give it rest. This
pseudo morgue humour. It's
tedious.

                    JEM
Okay. Answer me this then. When
should morgue humour be used? If
not in a situation of peril where
said humour becomes ironic.
Doctors use it all the time. It
lightens the pressure, babe.

                    THORNE
Call me 'babe' again, tosser and
I'll ...

Distant shots can be heard. Rat a Tat Tat. Someone
screams outside and the kids all look towards THE DOOR.

                    SUSIE
We should have a look through the
top window. See what's happening.

                    BEN
I'm not looking through the
window. I don't want to get my
head blown off.

                    THORNE
Any luck with the police? We need
an ambulance for Mr B. And any
other (pause) you know,
casualties.

                    THORNE
          We should move him out of the room
          or put him in a cupboard or
          something. If he turns while we
          are still in here ...

                    BEN
          What do you mean if he turns?

                    KIKO
          She means if he's infected by the
          zombie virus.

SUSIE looks at THORNE as if she is quite mad. THORNE just
shrugs.

                    SUSIE
          You are so weird.

                    THORNE
          I'd rather be weird than a Hannah
          Montana clone that pukes up her
          lunch every day. You know you have
          that taint of sick on your breath.
          It's disgusting. And you call me
          weird?

THORNE points her finger at her temple and twirls it
around.

                    KIKO
          Leave her alone.

                    THORNE
          The Japanese Geisha to the rescue?
          Wow! That's something right there.

                    KIKO
          Just stop it. Our teacher is dead
          and my Math test is delayed and
          I'm feeling really pissed off. My
          parents will *never believe* me. On
          a scale of 'my dog ate my
          homework' excuses - this is
          just...

                    SUSIE
          Random?

KIKO smiles at SUSIE gratefully.

KIKO
Yeah! Really random. My Dad willrequire proof. Police photographs or something.

SUSIE
But why? You're are an honours student. You'll probably graduate magna cum laude. What more can they possibly want from you.

KIKO
More. They always want more. And worse, they are such a cliche. That Asian drive towards perfection and achievement. And you know what? The little secret that my Dad has been hiding for years. His parents are from Hawaii. He doesn't even have Asian blood. This whole Japanese thing? The way he makes us live. A total charade. My mum's Irish!! But dyes her hair black.

SUSIE
No! Really?

KIKO
Yes, totally. She uses that hard core stuff. L'Oreal or something. (pause) But the weird thing is that the longer you are a part of the lie - the better you get at living it.

SUSIE
Why would your Dad do that? I mean it sounds exhausting. How does he not slip up and forget his back story? I have problems with tiny lies.

KIKO
He feels that Hawaiians have this rep for being laid back and unambitious and I guess he didn't want to be labelled as that. The Asian culture appealed to his drive.

SUSIE
But he's making you live a lie. I mean you are a Hula girl. You should be in a grass skirt, shaking your thang.

SUSIE and KIKO laugh.

                KIKO
      You think I'd look pretty in
      a hula skirt?

SUSIE looks up at KIKO.

                SUSIE
      I think you'd look pretty in
      anything.

SUSIE and KIKO stare at each other and then break off into grins.

                KIKO
      You want to go out after this is
      over? To the movies or something?
      Unless we are zombies by then.

                SUSIE
      We could still go out. Just be
      undead. Slight obstacle but
      nothing I can't handle.

                KIKO
      Yeah. Zombie dates rock.

                SUSIE
      So it would be a date?

                KIKO
      If you want?

SUSIE grins.

                SUSIE
      Okay, then.

                KIKO
      I've got great timing right?

                SUSIE
      What do you mean?

                KIKO
      It's not like we will ever forget
      the moment I asked you out.

This brings them back to earth with a bump and SUSIE bites

her lip looking anxious again. KIKO leans over and gives SUSIE a quick kiss on the cheek.

> KIKO (CONT'D)
> It's going to be okay.

> SUSIE
> How do you know?

> KIKO
> (shrugs) It has to be.

SUSIE nods and remembers Mr B. She moves to Mr B's body, pauses as if feeling for a pulse and then slumps.

> SUSIE
> No pulse. He's ... gone.

> JEM
> Told you.

> BEN
> Are you sure, SUSIE?

SUSIE just nods. The children are in stages of shock except for FANBOY who seems unconcerned.

> BEN (CONT'D)
> (Pulling himself together) Can someone call an ambulance or something.

> KIKO
> We heard sirens earlier perhaps they are already here.

> JEM
> I've go no signal. Nothing.

> THORNE
> Me too. Nothing.

THORNE AND JEM stare at each other.

> FANBOY
> I've blocked the signal. There is no point trying.

The children turn to face FANBOY accusatory and disbelieving looks.

                    JEM
          What did you say?

                    FANBOY
          The signal is blocked. We did it
          this morning. You won't get
          anything. I let you have a bit to
          contact the police and the press.
          But I've cut it off now.

JEM looks puzzled.

                    JEM
          Okay. So where's the signal
          blocker then? You have to have it
          near by, right? Otherwise it
          wouldn't be strong enough.

                    THORNE
          He's lying. He is always lying.
          It's like default mode or
          something.

Another shot rings out louder still and a scream.

The children crouch again looking towards THE DOOR.

MOTHER enters stage right and stands upstage right facing the audience.

                    MOTHER
          How can the school let this
          happen? We have had the warnings,
          haven't we? Other kids lost to
          other bullets or prison sentences
          or worse. A flash of self-
          indulgence peppered with a bit of
          sociopath and it all becomes red.
          And then black. And we, the
          survivors, if you can call us
          that, because we don't survive
          really. We exist, we cope. We
          wait for things. Always waiting
          for holidays to pass quickly under
          the bedclothes or huddled in their
          bedroom closet clutching that
          shabby bear they have loved since
          birth. Special days to drown in
          bottles of brandy or cheap, red
          wine. We, the survivors, become
          addicts of every kind. Hand in
          hand with Dr Phil as he bleats and

craps his pop psychology all over the world. We are the faithless faithful. Our church has become Fox television and we are betraying our kid's childhoods with programmes as tenuous as dandelion fluff.

MOTHER exits stage right.

          FANBOY
(Smiling broadly) Not lying. Blocker is outside the room. Hidden under a bush. The explosions you heard earlier. A diversion courtesy of Mr Harris and Klebold. (checks his watch). It's all going well so far.

          BEN
What the hell are you talking about, you freak? Mr Harris and who?

          THORNE
He's talking about the Columbine shooters. The boys that did it. Eric and Dylan.

          BEN
(angry - fists clenched) What?

          JEM
BEN, don't. Let's hear what the lame ass has to say? Come on, then you've got the floor. Whatever the fantasy - lets have it. Just one question. How long have you been on the medication, psycho?

FANBOY keep smiling as he places a handgun on the desk in front of him. SUSIE gasps and the other kids take a step backwards.

          KIKO
Is that for real? It's not a replica or anything.

          FANBOY
The real thing. Fully loaded, automatic. Ready to go. Licensed to kill anybody so I advise you all to shut the fuck up and listen.

FANBOY looks hard at each of the students. BEN seems about to say or do something but backs down. JEM just shrugs. KIKO looks unruffled and SUSIE puts her face in her hands.

                    FANBOY (CONT'D)
Listen up. My associate is currently balancing her books. The only thing that is standing between you and her and (pause) death. Is me. I have this flag in my bag. If I decide to hang it on the door knob outside then my associate will come in and start to spray bullets like a 1980's action star.

                    JEM
Very fucking dramatic.

                    SUSIE
Her? He said her, right?

                    FANBOY
Yeah? So what? You think a girl can't be a hard ass? A girl can't be a mass murderer?

                    SUSIE
No, no, Of course. I just ... It's unexpected that's all. (Pause) Who is it?

                    KIKO
I bet it's Christa. Such a freakazoid.

                    BEN
Well, she may be weird but she wouldn't kill anybody.

                    SUSIE
She gets teased a lot about her zits.

                    FANBOY
By you.

SUSIE says nothing. Her head falls.

                    FANBOY (CONT'D)
But it's not her.

FANBOY stares intently at JEM.

                JEM
(Quietly)Oh, Shit. It's MEGAN, isn't it.

              FANBOY
(In a quiz show host voice)
And the prize goes to the brother whose twin sister is on a killing spree.

JEM starts out of his chair, his face puce with rage.

                JEM
What have you done? WHAT HAVE YOU DONE?

              FANBOY
Me? Nothing. I'm just sitting here being friendly. I'm not responsible for your sister and her sociopathic tendencies. However, I do admire them.

                JEM
What bullshit have you been feeding her?

              FANBOY
Hey, she's a very sad young lady. Very sad and full of rage. Really doesn't like your parents much. I bet she's a handful at Christmas. Thanksgiving must be a blast.

                JEM
I'm going to kill you.

              FANBOY
(Waves gun around) Have a go. Go on. MEGAN would be so proud.
(Pause) You know what we need? Some music. Tunes to kill by.

FANBOY fiddles about in his rucksack pulling out a bicycle lock and a small, portable speaker. He hooks up the system and an angry sounding band start to play. The music is very loud and FANBOY starts grinning at THE DOOR. The other kids watch him and then BEN lunges for the speaker.

                BEN
It's a signal. He's telling Megan to come in.

BEN grabs the speaker and tears out the cord.

> FANBOY
> Getting paranoid, Ben?

> SUSIE
> (Quietly) Why is she doing this, Dougie? Why is Megan killing everyone?

> FANBOY
> (Angry) Don't call me that.

> THORNE
> It's your name.

> FANBOY
> Not anymore. In the papers tomorrow it will be FANBOY - School Shooter.

> SUSIE
> You haven't shot anyone yet.

> FANBOY
> There's still time, SUSIE. And the twatting liberals will bleat on about 'why did it happen" and 'What went wrong?.

> SUSIE
> What did go wrong?

> FANBOY
> (Shrugs) Nothing went wrong. I have great, loving parents. So bloody great and so bloody loving. Everything I do is a minor celebration. I got a D - OMG let's go to Mauritius for 2 weeks.

FANBOY slams the gun down.

> FANBOY (CONT'D)
> I have everything I want. Ipad, Ipod, AirBook, TV, PS2, XBox. And a lovely kindle to read from. Do you know that you can learn how to make a bomb and steal someone's identity in a couple of clicks. (Adopts gruff voice). You want to tickets to the game, Son? Here

take 10. Borrow the car for the week. Never mind that fender. Everybody has accidents right. He didn't mean to hurt his sister. It's boisterous play. Boy's will be boys.

                    JEM
          Sounds pretty good to me.

                    FANBOY
          Does it? Everything you do.
          Every statement you make is
          fucking understood. Treated with
          compassion and
          empathy. It drives me nuts.

FANBOY stands up and moves to the desk.

                    FANBOY (CONT'D)
          I need to do something that they
          will never understand. That they
          will be haunted by night after
          dark, dark night.

                    THORNE
          Play the tiny violin for the poor,
          over indulged little tool. Wah
          Wah Wah. Jesus Christ.

                    BEN
          Thorne, don't.

                    THORNE
          It's got nothing to do with his
          background, BEN. Don't you see?
          All this drama and stuff. He
          thinks he's eternal. He actually
          thinks nothing can touch him. But
          when the Feds come busting through
          the door and blow his brains out
          all over the wall, then he might
          think differently.

THORNE spits on the floor in front of FANBOY.

                    THORNE (CONT'D)
          You make me want to puke. And
          I ..

FANBOY raises the gun and shoots THORNE who falls to her knees and then the floor.

                    FANBOY
          (giggles) Ooops.

MOTHER enters stage right and stands upstage right facing audience.

                    MOTHER
          And my love, my Sasha, lies there.
          Under a table in the library.
          Breathless and wheezy as the dust
          motes from a thousand books
          experiment with flight as bullets
          rock the air beside them. And her
          pain, my pain which twins and
          melds the golden cord that starts
          at conception between mother and
          child turns crimson and breaks
          like cheap, cotton thread past its
          best. And the hours and minutes
          and years of the lies - of us
          telling them that we will always
          stand tall and fierce and protect
          them from the monsters. From the
          bad things, from the creatures of
          the night that languish under beds
          and in cupboards and behind the
          bookshelf. Nothing bad. Ever.
          Will happen. Until it does. And
          that lie is brandished by us all.
          And it is worse than betrayal
          because our children believe us
          and strut about this world with a
          heady confidence that ultimately
          ends them. Cutting through their
          innocence or their dreams or
          bodies and creating an emotional
          extinction event. Ground zero for
          out children. It is now. Here.

MOTHER picks up her bag and keys and starts to exit stage. She pauses and turns back to the audience.

                    MOTHER (CONT'D)
          I think of her now, as she was at
          five, dancing in the breaker
          waves. Her skin salty as butter
          and her wind-whipped hair pulling
          the sky towards her. Sand-dollar
          eyes filling with beauty and
          wonder. And I recorded it in my

> heart and it became a piece of my daughter's history. I will not countenance another. I will not.

A shocked silence before KIKO and SUSIE scream and hug each other. BEN slumps into a chair, his mouth slack. Only JEM moves quickly to THORNE's body and listens for a heartbeat.

JEM looks up at BEN and shakes his head. BEN, his fists clenched walks away from them all and stand on the other side of the room.

SUSIE and KIKO hold each other. SUSIE sobs quietly but KIKO stares over the top of her head at FANBOY.

> KIKO
> What do you want? What do you think is going to happen here?

> FANBOY
> Well, I have to admit that was unexpected but she was annoying the fuck out of me. So pretentious. I mean changing your name to Thorne in homage to vampires that sparkle in the daylight. She could have got Harry Styles tattooed on her back. That, at least, would have been more contemporary.

> KIKO
> You shot her...(pause)... Because you were bored?

> FANBOY
> Basically, yes. And the moles on her face. Moles are creepy.

FANBOY shudders.

> KIKO
> I can't believe this. It's like (bemused)... It's like... I don't know what it's like. I've no point of reference for this at all. I think I'm going mad.

> FANBOY
> Madness is relative. I mean, this might be described as insanity. Megan out there going postal and me in here, you know, 'deciding'.

                    BEN
          I don't think you are mad at all.
          Your brain is disconnected or
          something.

                    FANBOY
          My brain is just fine, dude. None
          of you realised what MEGAN and I
          were planning. None of you know
          what we are going to do next.
          We've outsmarted everybody.
          Teachers, parents, police,
          shrinks. All those fuckers. Our
          legacy will be carved into history
          for ever. None will ever forget
          this day.

                    JEM
          Your legacy will be the death
          penalty. You get fried in this
          country and don't think they won't
          try you as an adult, 'dude'.

                    FANBOY
          If I go down, your precious MEGAN
          goes down too. You know nothing
          about her do you. You've been her
          twin for 15 years and you had no
          idea she was planning this. NO
          IDEA that she has this bad ass,
          ice cold blood. Do you know how
          many times she has talked about
          killing you? What a drag you are.
          How Emo you are. What lame music
          you listen to. She fucking hates
          you.

JEM is silent. He stands staring at FANBOY. The lack of
expression on his face is mesmerising.

                    FANBOY (cont'D)
          Your, Dad? Paragon of the
          community and friend to all has
          been touching her in all sorts of
          nasty ways since she was 7. Yeah,
          Mr Christian Morals is a paedo.

FANBOY is almost hysterical now. His voice rising in
pitch.

                    JEM (quietly)
              That didn't happen. I would
              know. We shared a room until we
              were ten.
              You. Are. A. Liar.

FANBOY deflates quickly.

                    FANBOY
              Yes. (copies JEM's words. I. AM.
              A. LIAR... (pause) ... so perhaps
              it's not Megan out there. Perhaps
              it's the ghost of Dylan Klebold
              and his Trench Coat Mafia.

Screams punch the air but die out quickly.

SUSIE moans to herself. KIKO hugs her gently.

                    FANBOY (CONT'D)
              Looks like they are warming up to
              the main event.

                    BEN
              Fuck you. Jem, help me move
              Thorne's...er... Thorne
              over there.

BEN points to the covered area where MR B's body is lying.
JEM wipes his hands on his jeans as if they are sweaty and
joins BEN. They move THORNE'S body gently to the covered
area.

                    BEN (CONT'D)
              We have to do something. I can't
              wait to see if I get shot or not.
              Anyone of us could be next. The
              freak has completely lost it.

                    JEM
              I don't think he has. This was
              really well organised. I think we
              are safe until he gets bored with
              us.

                    BEN
              Are you suggesting we entertain
              him? I mean I can tap dance a
              little but ..

                    JEM
              (snorts softly) No, you idiot.
              Although, I'd pay to see that.

BEN mouths a profanity at JEM.

JEM (CONT'D)
Actually, I don't think we have any control over it at all. We could try to rush him but he might be hooked up to something. He might have placed explosives anywhere. The psycho has had months/years to perfect this.

BEN
So what do you suggest?

JEM
When I think of something I'll let you know.

BEN
Do you think it's really Megan out there?

JEM
Probably. Psycho was right about her being angry. I don't know why. But she's never talked to me about killing the folks. I mean she is my best friend. You can't keep that kind of rage hidden from your twin.

BEN
Meg has never struck me as angry. Just sort of insubstantial. Like you took all the colour from her in the womb or something. I mean, she's smart and quite cute ...

JEM
Dude, that's my sister.

BEN
Hey, I'm just saying that she has never seemed that angry. Have you noticed anything?

JEM
She cuts herself on her thighs. Maybe her arms too. I haven't seen those. I read that this is a sign of suppressed, you know, rage. Our parents have no idea. So busy being Super People in the Neighbourhood. We just exist on

the edge of their relationship. I
think they only had us because it
was the 'thing' to do. Like tennis
lessons or something. Mum's okay
when she is on her own. She can
be fun, you know, silly and shit.
But my Dad is a total prick. He
doesn't even pretend to be a Dad
in the home. Sometimes he looks
at us and it's like he doesn't
recognise who we are. Who I am.
It's weird. Like he knows us but
in this very distant way. But Meg
and I have always had each other
so I'd know, right, if anything
had changed. I'd feel it.

              BEN

Yep, twins have that whole
closeness thing.

              JEM

It's more than that. We are
mirror image twins. So even Meg's
organs are on the opposite to
mine. We both have strawberry
marks on our necks ... (points to
neck) ... but hers are on the
other side. Our noses are
slightly crooked but off at
opposing angles. So I would know.
I really would.

            FANBOY

Hurry it up!

              JEM

(whispers) I'd know.

JEM and BEN move back to the desks but while BEN takes the furthest one from the front, JEM sits as near to FANBOY as he can. And continues to stare.

            FANBOY

I know. Let's play a game. Let's
play musical chairs with a twist.

              JEM

Fuck you.

FANBOY
I never knew you cared? Right line four chairs up. No. Three, sorry. Cos' Thorne, you know, is sorta dead.

More shots ring out. FANBOY's face screws up a bit.

FANBOY (CONT'D)
Exciting! Right this is how it goes. I'm going to play some music and you are going to dance around - not lame arse dancing - I want rhythm, people. And when the music stops - the person still standing is *disqualified*

FANBOY does air quotes using both hands one of which is holding the hand gun when saying 'disqualified'.

FANBOY (CONT'D)
There are a few more rules. If you bore me you are disqualified. If you shuffle or do 'sad dad at a wedding' dancing - you are disqualified. If you look sad or scared - disqualified. (pause) Are we clear?

The rest of the kids stare at him unable to decide if he is joking or not.

FANBOY sighs dramatically and points the gun to the ceiling and shoots. There are screams and shouts and the kids run to the centre of the room and start to organise 4 chairs.

FANBOY (CONT'D)
Put them back to back. That's it.

BEN
He *is* mad. We don't stand a chance. He is going to kill us all.

JEM
I've got a plan. Just let me be the one still standing when the music stops.

BEN
But...

                    JEM
          Not much to lose really and I
          needto know if Megan is
          outside. I have to help her.

Sirens screech in background.

                    JEM (CONT'D)
          The police ... you know what
          they'll do.

BEN nods.
                    BEN
          Thanks, man.

JEM shrugs.

Weird, creepy music starts up from FANBOY's Ipod but
something with a punchy rhythm. The kids start to move
around the chairs - hopelessly awkward trying to shimmy and
move in time to the music. This is an exercise in
humiliation. The sadistic nuns did it to the unmarried
mothers in Southern Ireland. And the Nazi's. (see The
Pianist).

SUSIE is sobbing with fear and embarrassment. KIKO's face
remains impassive apart from her eyes that blink furiously.
BEN and JEM move just intent on staying alive.

                    KIKO
          This is so humiliating. It's like
          the film about the Nazis. You
          know, when they make those old
          people dance for them. In the
          camp.

                    JEM
          I think that's the point.

FANBOY shouts encouragement from behind the desk - banging
the gun on the desk enthusiastically.

When the music stops suddenly there is a scramble for the
chairs. BEN, SUSIE and KIKO find seats. Relief and guilt
present on their faces. JEM remains standing having made
no effort to grab one.

FANBOY and JEM stare at each other for a split second and
then JEM grabs the nearest chair and flings it at FANBOY.
It doesn't knock him over but distracts him enough to drop
the gun. FANBOY and JEM both lunge for the gun and wrestle
on the floor.

The other kids mobilise and SUSIE looks around for weapon
and uses a wastepaper bin to hit FANBOY until he starts
to go limp.

JEM has FANBOY in a hold. SUSIE takes a step back breathing heavily.

The handle on THE DOOR to the corridor begins to turn from side to side as someone is trying to open it.

JEM points the gun at the door as it begins to open and MEGAN, JEM's twin, appears in the doorway holding a sawn off shotgun.

                    JEM (CONT'D)
    Meg?

MEGAN ignores him and addresses FANBOY.

                    MEGAN
    I told you that he wasn't to be
    involved.

                    FANBOY
    (holding mouth) He was here
    already. Nothing I could do.

                    MEGAN
    I told you to send him out. He's
    not part of this.

MEGAN turns to JEM

                    MEGAN (CONT'D)
    You are not part of this, Jem.

                    JEM
    How can you say that? I'm part of
    it by default. (pause) I'm not
    going to ask why, Meg, but I'm
    stopping it now.

                    MEGAN
    It's a bit too late for that,
    Twin. There is a big mess out
    there. I knew going into this
    that I wouldn't be coming out.
    You know, that this was a one way
    trip. I never intended to come
    out alive. I don't think its
    possible really.

                    JEM
    Meg. We'll do it together. I won't
    leave you. I'm not letting you go
    out there alone.

MEGAN lowers her gun.

>   MEGAN
> I'm so tired. I can't think beyond
> this moment. The police have
> arrived. They're everywhere. I
> suppose I should be proud that
> I've achieved this kind of
> attention.

>   SUSIE
> He was going to kill us. One by
> One. He already shot Thorne.

>   Megan
> (shrugs) I promised him some
> collateral. But not Jem. That
> was never the deal. (To FANBOY)
> You should have sent him out.
> Through the window. Anything. But
> you didn't. Why?

>   FANBOY
> (shrugs) JEM was my insurance in
> case you thought it might be a
> good idea to change plans. Like
> blame it all on me or something.

>   MEGAN
> (laughs) Where has the trust gone?
> Anyway, it's over now. I don't
> have the energy for anything else.
> You should all leave.

The kids get up and begin to file out slowly.

>   MEGAN (CONT'D)
> (shouts) Remember to keep you
> hands above your heads! High so
> the police can see.

MEGAN looks at JEM

>   MEGAN (CONT'D)
> You should go too.

>   JEM
> I will. With you.

>   MEGAN
> Jem, no.

JEM
Think about it? There's no going back and I can't stay in the same place without you. (smiles) You don't want to condemn me to years and years of heartache do you?

MEGAN give him a 'come off it' look.

JEM (CONT'D)
So, we move forward. Together. Okay?

MEGAN
What about him? (points at FANBOY)

JEM
He's our hostage.

MEGAN
You know what's going to happen.

JEM
I've got a reasonable idea, yes.

MEGAN
Do you think it will hurt?

JEM
I expect it will be very quick.

MEGAN
But do you think it will hurt (laughs nervously) I'm not very good with pain.

JEM
But you cut yourself.

MEGAN
Oh! You know about that.

JEM
Of course, I do.

MEGAN
It's a different type of pain. Like I'm almost numb with grief when I do it. It hurts - but I feel so much better. Free. Like I've let something poisonous out. Something toxic.

JEM smiles sadly.

                JEM
I remember you being a complete wuss when you were little. I have Two Words for, Marco & Polo!

                MEGAN
That is so unfair. I was, like, six!

                JEM (smiling)
You cried. Like little girl kittens.

                MEGAN
Hey! A broken wrist really hurts.

                JEM
I know, I'm just kidding.

                MEGAN
(anxious again) Will it hurt like that?

                JEM
(quietly) No, I don't think it will hurt at all.

JEM and MEGAN smile at each other fondly.

                FANBOY
Hey! I'm not just going to walk out of here with my hands up. You are not having all the glory. I want my 15 minutes. You promised me my 15 minutes!

                MEGAN
(wearily) Shut up!

                JEM
Did you have to kill Mrs. Williamson?

                MEGAN
Yeah, sorry about that. I just got a bit carried away. Once I started. It's like beginning a huge tub of ice cream. It's really difficult to stop eating.

                    JEM
               Really?

                    MEGAN
               Seriously.

                    JEM
               Right. Okay, you ready?

MEGAN nods and gestures the gun towards FANBOY.

                    MEGAN
                On your feet, School Shooter.

FANBOY struggles to his feet and walks towards THE DOOR.

                    JEM
               Love you, Meg.

                    MEGAN
               Love you back, twin.

JEM and MEGAN walk out of the room together. THE DOOR is open - several seconds late we hear two distinct shots.

END

www.ingramcontent.com/pod-product-compliance
Lightning Source LLC
Chambersburg PA
CBHW070051070426
42449CB00012BA/3225